Den Chief Handbook

DEN CHIEF

BOY SCOUTS OF AMERICA

33211A
ISBN 0-8395-3211-3
©1998 Boy Scouts of America
Revised 1999

10   9   8   7   6   5   4   3   2

Contents

CHAPTER 1

You and
the Den

Your Scoutmaster and senior patrol leader have selected you to be a den chief. This makes you a leader in your troop and a leader of Cub Scouts. As den chief, you have the opportunity to do a Good Turn for younger boys who will look up to you and want to be like you. To them, you are the Boy Scouts.

Leadership

What is leadership? Leadership means responsibility. It's adventure and often fun, but it always means responsibility. The leader is the person others look to, to get the job done. Don't think your new job as a leader will be just an honor. It's much more than that. It means that the other Scouts expect you to take the responsibility of getting the job done.

You were selected because you have the potential for being a leader. How well you do will be mostly up to you. Others will help you. And you'll have fun.

As den chief, you should set a good example for younger boys. Through you they will learn what it means to be a Boy Scout. Being den chief is an important position; therefore, you should not hold another leadership position in your troop while you are serving as den chief.

Cub Scouting is a family program, and you'll meet the families of your den members. These people will be grateful to you when they see how much their sons like you and look up to you. Being a den chief is your chance to be an example and a real leader. You'll have fun teaching

Cub Scouts things you know. And you'll feel good when they ask you for help and advice.

You'll be a big help to den leaders. They will count on you to be responsible and reliable. You'll learn from them also. You'll have the chance to use some of your ideas to plan things, and help make them happen.

As den chief, you are a leader. You are in the den so that Cub Scouts and Webelos Scouts will have a real, live Boy Scout helping them. They'll want to be like you. They'll be eager to become Boy Scouts when they are old enough. Because of you, when they are Boy Scouts, they'll find it easier to work with boy leaders as well as with adult leaders.

Part of being a leader is being reliable. The den leader is expecting you to be at den and pack meetings. If you cannot be at a meeting, be sure to contact the leader ahead of time so that other arrangements can be made. Den leaders know that you are busy. But they also know that you have made a commitment and plan to honor it.

You'll go on interesting trips and participate in activities with your den and pack. You'll have many more experiences than the other boys in your troop. Your job in the den plus your being a Boy Scout in your troop will keep you busy, but busy people get things done.

Insignia

Wear your badge of office proudly. Your troop will present you with the den chief badge, which you'll wear on the left sleeve of your uniform. The Cub Scout pack will give you the den chief cord, which is worn on your left shoulder.

When you have completed den chief training conducted by your district or council or pack, you are eligible to wear the "Trained" emblem below your den chief badge of office.

Den Chief

**Webelos
Den Chief**

Den Chief Service Award

The Den Chief Service Award recognizes den chiefs who lead and serve their dens for at least a year. This award emphasizes your key role within Boy Scouting—and compliments you for your important service.

What do you have to do for the award? This book tells you what you must be and do to become an outstanding den chief. In Chapter 6, you'll find the requirements for this award. Use this book as a guide to meeting these requirements.

Den Chief Pledge

This is a good time to read the pledge so that you will know and understand what is expected of you.

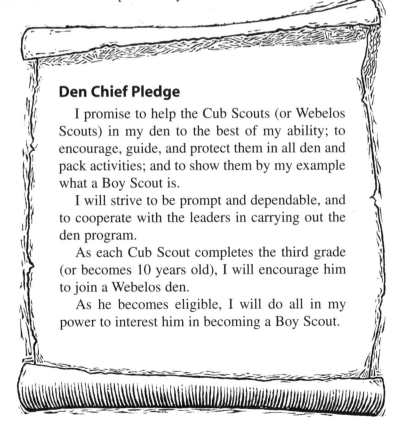

Den Chief Pledge

I promise to help the Cub Scouts (or Webelos Scouts) in my den to the best of my ability; to encourage, guide, and protect them in all den and pack activities; and to show them by my example what a Boy Scout is.

I will strive to be prompt and dependable, and to cooperate with the leaders in carrying out the den program.

As each Cub Scout completes the third grade (or becomes 10 years old), I will encourage him to join a Webelos den.

As he becomes eligible, I will do all in my power to interest him in becoming a Boy Scout.

Supervision and Training

As den chief, you are responsible to the den leaders in your pack and to the person in your troop who serves as den chief coordinator. This may be your junior assistant Scoutmaster or your assistant Scoutmaster.

This handbook will help you understand your duties. You'll learn as you work with your den and pack leaders. Assistant Cubmasters usually are responsible for helping den chiefs. There is also den chief training that you should attend. And there are meetings where the pack program is planned.

If you cannot attend your district or council den chief training, your den leader and the assistant Cubmaster may conduct training for you.

How Cub Scouting Is Organized

Cub Scouting is organized around dens. There are Tiger Cub dens for boys in the first grade (or who are age 7). Tiger Cub dens do not use den chiefs.

Cub Scout dens are for boys in the second and third grades (or ages 8 and 9). All boys who become Cub Scouts or Webelos Scouts first learn the eight things that lead to the Bobcat badge. Cub Scouts work on achievements and electives to earn the Wolf and Bear badges, as well as gold and silver arrow points. Most of these are done at home with their parents, but some things are done in den meetings.

Webelos Scout dens are for boys in the fourth and fifth grades (or age 10). Webelos Scouts can earn up to 20 activity badges. Most activity badge requirements are completed at den meetings and approved by the Webelos leader, or someone appointed by the Webelos leader. In addition, Webelos Scouts learn many of the things that are needed to become Boy Scouts. Their recognition is the Webelos badge and the Arrow of Light Award, the highest rank a Webelos Scout can earn.

Most dens meet every week, usually for about an hour. You'll be very involved with the den meetings, including helping to plan them.

The pack meeting—a meeting of all the dens and the families of the Tiger Cubs, Cub Scouts, and Webelos Scouts—takes place once a month. You'll also attend these meetings and help with your den's participation in the program.

The next few chapters include details of all of these meetings and your responsibilities. To do your best as a den chief, it is important that you use this book to learn all you can to help Cub Scouts and Webelos Scouts and their leaders.

CHAPTER 2

Responsibilities of Den Chiefs

Now, let's look at the job of being a den chief. First, you need to know some things about the Cub Scout program. The next two chapters will get into the details of being a den chief either to Cub Scouts, who are in the second and third grades, or to Webelos Scouts, who are in the fourth and fifth grades.

It will be helpful if you are two, three, or four years older than the boys with whom you will be working in the den.

Duties of Den Chiefs

The duties of all den chiefs are:

- Know the purposes of Cub Scouting.
- Help Cub Scouts achieve the purposes of Cub Scouting.
- Be the activities assistant in den meetings.
- Set a good example by attitude and uniforming.
- Take part in weekly den meetings.
- Assist the den in its part of the monthly pack meeting program.
- Be a friend to the boys in the den.
- Know the importance of the monthly theme.
- Meet as needed with the adult members of the den, pack, and troop.

Know the Purposes of Cub Scouting

Cub Scouting is a program of the Boy Scouts of America for parents, leaders, and organizations to use with boys in first through fifth grades (or 7, 8, 9, and 10 years of age) for the purposes of:

1. Influencing the development of character and encouraging spiritual growth

2. Helping boys develop habits and attitudes of good citizenship

3. Encouraging good sportsmanship and pride in mind and body

4. Improving understanding within the family

5. Strengthening boys' ability to get along with other boys and respect other people

6. Fostering a sense of personal achievement by helping boys develop new interests and skills

7. Showing how to be helpful and do one's best

8. Providing fun and exciting new things for boys to do

9. Preparing them to become Boy Scouts

Talk with your den leader about the meaning of each point. It is the job of the adults in Cub Scouting to see that the nine points are achieved. Your job is to help.

Help Cub Scouts Achieve the Purposes of Cub Scouting

Cub Scouting is a year-round program of action, achievement, healthfulness, and helpfulness. Through the program, a boy is taught respect for his God, his country, his home, and other people. He is also given opportunities to take part in activities and to do things for others—a vital part of good citizenship.

Everything you do to help the den leader and the Cub Scouts will help make these things happen. As you learn more about the things that go on in a den and a pack, you'll see how this happens. For the moment, just try to understand the purpose.

As a Boy Scout you have to know the Scout Oath, Law, and motto. Well, Cub Scouts have to learn similar things, too. All Cub Scouts have to earn the Bobcat badge. To do that they must know the following things. You should know these, too, and then help Cub Scouts learn them.

Cub Scout Promise

I, [name], promise to do my best
To do my duty to God and my country,
To help other people, and
To obey the Law of the Pack.

Law of the Pack

The Cub Scout follows Akela.
The Cub Scout helps the pack go.
The pack helps the Cub Scout grow.
The Cub Scout gives goodwill.

Cub Scout Motto

Do Your Best.

Cub Scout Salute

Cub Scout Sign

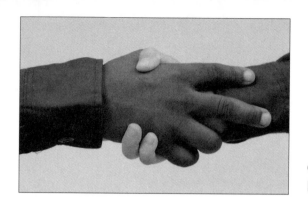

**Cub Scout
Handshake**

Tell what Webelos Means

Webelos: Say WEE-buh-lows.
It means <u>WE</u>'ll <u>BE</u> <u>LO</u>yal <u>S</u>couts.

Be the Activities Assistant

The best place to get help in learning how to be the activities assistant is at den chief training. This is a meeting that you can go to with your Cubmaster and den leaders. The person in your troop who serves as the den chief coordinator should go to this meeting, too.

Training will make you more effective in your leadership role. You'll find it easier to do your job. You'll have know-how!

Many other den chiefs and their leaders will be at this training. Activities will teach you what every den chief needs to know. But until this training takes place, you need to know a few things about how to lead activities. You'll find many ideas in Chapter 5, "Den Chief Ideas Chest."

LEADING SONGS. Leading songs can be fun. You don't have to be a great singer or conductor. Just show enthusiasm! Here are some hints to help you get started:

- Pick a song to suit the meeting. Practice the words and music ahead of time.

- Start with a smile. Let the boys know this is going to be fun.

- Hum the song softly to yourself to get the pitch.

- Use easy-to-follow hand movements to indicate start, faster, slower, softer, louder.

- Run through the song and words with the den once for practice.

LEADING STUNTS AND SKITS. Here are some tips for leading stunts and skits.

- Encourage the boys to come up with their own ideas.

- Help prepare the script. Help select a narrator. Work with boys to select their parts.

- Try pantomime—telling a story or spelling out words without speaking.

- Coach the boys in the parts they are playing.

- Help them make costumes, puppets, or props.

LEADING GAMES. Cub Scouts like to play action games.

- Suit the game to the room and space available. It will have to be a less-active game if the den meeting is in a home or small room.

- Explain the rules of the game and encourage boys to follow the rules and play fairly.

- Help boys who are disabled take part in the games.

- Use games that will help boys in advancement.

- Be the referee or the judge, if needed.

LEADING SPORTS. You may know a lot more about sports than the Cub Scouts in your den. It's a good idea to be certain that you know the rules. When you are asked, you might:

- Lead a game of baseball, soccer, or stickball; or set up a relay race.

- Help in coaching the den in one or more Cub Scout sports.

- Do physical fitness exercises if you don't have the space for a very active game.

Set a Good Example

People give an impression of the kind of person they are in many ways. You set a good example by how you look, how you wear your uniform, and how you speak as well as by your pride in being a Boy Scout. Cub Scouts want to be like you.

Remember: Through your example and attitude, you are always leading. The boys look up to you unless you show them, by things you do or say, that they should not look up to you.

ATTITUDE. Attitude is how you feel about yourself, about people, and about things. It is whether you raise your voice to make a point or whether you speak quietly and still get your ideas across. It is showing that you like what you are doing. It is liking yourself as a person but not being conceited.

If you come to den meetings in a grumpy mood, you can spoil the meeting for your Cub Scouts. Sure, you may not always feel great, but try not to show it. You may even feel better yourself as you try not to show your bad mood.

Try to be cheerful and happy when you are with your Cub Scouts. They came to have fun!

Attitude is also how you deal with adults. Speak politely to the den leaders. If you have a suggestion, speak up but don't insist on having your own way. If you disagree about something, say so politely and then make your own suggestions.

The Scout Law sums up very well what your attitude should be: trustworthy, loyal, helpful, friendly, courteous, kind, obedient, cheerful, thrifty, brave, clean, and reverent.

UNIFORMING. One way to set a good example is in the way you wear your Boy Scout uniform. Be neat and clean. Be in proper uniform for the meeting or activity. If you wear your neckerchief neatly, your Cub Scouts will be more likely to wear theirs that way, too.

Studies show that boys of Cub Scout age like to wear uniforms. They will like to see you dressed in your Scout uniform. What you do means a lot to them, so be sure to wear your uniform to every den and pack meeting, as well as other Cub Scout activities. If your den meets in the afternoon, you could carry your Scout uniform to school the day of your den meeting, or you could drop it off at the den's meeting place the day before the meeting.

Take Part in Den Meetings

A Cub Scout den has second- and third-grade boys in it. A Webelos den has boys who are in fourth and fifth grades. Six or eight boys may be in one den. The number of boys depends on how many the den leader can work with easily and the size of the meeting place. The den meets each week. Usually it meets in a den leader's home or in a school, a church, or a community building. The den meets whenever it is convenient for the adult leaders. It could be in the afternoon after school, in the evening after the adults get home from work, or on a weekend.

The den leader will need to know your school schedule and when your troop meets so that the time is good for you, too. You should try not to miss any den meetings. If you must miss a meeting, let the den leader know ahead of time.

You do your leadership job at den meetings. You help the boys advance in rank. You help them make things and you lead activities. You help get them ready for their part in the pack meeting.

Assist With the Pack Meeting Program

A Cub Scout pack is made up of dens, just as a troop is made up of patrols. Once each month, all the dens in a pack come together for a pack meeting. This meeting is led by a Cubmaster. At the pack meeting, the boys in each den get to show what they have been doing or making. There may be exhibits of the things boys have made. One den may put on a stunt or a skit. Another den may conduct a ceremony. It's a chance for everyone to take part.

Families of Cub Scouts are encouraged to come to pack meetings. It is at these meetings, in front of their families, that Cub Scouts receive recognition. This could be the awarding of a badge. It could be to honor a boy for some special achievement at school or in his community. Or it could be to recognize him for doing a service project.

At the pack meetings you'll meet other den chiefs like yourself. This is a good chance for you to exchange ideas and experiences.

At the pack meeting, you may be asked to help in several ways. Your den leader may need you to get the boys and their families seated in their assigned places. You help your den do whatever it was asked to do for the meeting, such as:

- Put on a skit.

- Conduct the opening or closing ceremony.

- Lead a song.

Just be ready to pitch in and help in any way. And keep an eye on your boys to see that they behave.

Be a Friend

You know the meaning of friendship. You have many friends of your own age. You like to do things together. But can you be a friend to younger boys? Here are some tips to help you understand and get along with Cub Scouts:

- Boys at this age do not like to be made fun of or made to look silly.

- They worry a lot about what people think of them.

- They might appear not to listen to you the first time because they are testing you to see whether you mean what you say.

- They are big on rules. If you tell them what the rules are, they will try to obey them.

- They know when they have misbehaved and will expect you to say something.

- They want to be independent. They want to try things for themselves.

- They want to belong to a group so the boys in their den will become their friends.

- They read at different levels. One boy may read well and understand what is in his Cub Scout books. Another boy may be a poor reader and will need help. Don't embarrass the poor readers.

- They will not all be able to express themselves well. Some boys will talk more easily with you than other boys.

- They want to be active and to do physical things like running, jumping, and climbing.

- They have lots of energy and need good ways to use it.

- They will try to keep themselves neat and clean if you ask them.

- They need to be praised and made to feel good about things they have done.

- They can be asked to do things and be expected to get the job done.

- They love to compete with each other. If they lose or fail at something, they may need a little comforting. Their feelings are hurt easily.

- They love to talk about things they have done.

- They like to play action games with boys their own age.

- They are beginning to be interested in hobbies and in collecting things.

- They are close to their parents and care a lot about what their family thinks of them.

- They like their parents and family to do things with them.

Know the Importance of the Monthly Theme

Each month the program in your pack is based on a theme on which den and pack activities are built. The theme gives Cub Scouts new and interesting things to do.

For example, one month the theme may be "circus." In den meetings, the Cub Scouts might make costumes or plan a circus skit. They may play circus games or prepare a circus stunt for the pack meeting.

The theme gives everyone in a boy's family a chance to help. The family may help the boy make a costume or poster. As the boy works on his part in the theme, he is also able to earn credit toward achievements and electives or activity badges.

The den leader will tell you what the theme is. You, the den leader, and the boys plan what they want to do or make. This is where you can be a big help. You can teach the boys a game, trick, or song that fits the theme.

Meet With Adult Leaders

There are several times when you will meet with adults. Often these meetings are on the same dates as your regular den or pack meetings. It may sound like a lot of meetings, but it really isn't. You see your den leaders every week. You may meet for 10 minutes before or after each den meeting. Or you and the den leader may plan for the den meeting over the phone. It's a good idea to make notes to be sure you don't forget what you have been asked to do.

You can enter these plans in a special notebook (or your copy of the "Cub Scout Leader Program Notebook") that you will keep during the time you are a den chief. This is one of the requirements for the Den Chief Service Award. It also helps you keep track of the plans for each den meeting.

The Cubmaster or assistant Cubmaster may want to have a few minutes with you and other den chiefs before or after the pack meeting.

In your troop, you may have an occasional meeting with the person who serves as den chief coordinator.

One important meeting for every pack is the annual program planning conference. This is usually held in the late summer. At this conference, leaders of a pack decide the theme for each month of the year. Pack trips and activities may be planned. Summertime pack activities will be decided. You should go to this meeting with your den leaders so that you are a part of the plans the pack makes for the whole year. It is important that you know when pack meetings and activities will be so you can put them on your personal calendar.

CHAPTER 3

The Cub Scout Den Chief

In your position as den chief of a Cub Scout den, you can help in many ways.

Duties of Cub Scout Den Chiefs

- Help at den meetings.
- Assist Cub Scouts with the advancement plan.
- Help the denner and assistant denner to be leaders.
- Encourage Cub Scouts to become Webelos Scouts.

Help at Den Meetings

You help the den leader as you are asked. Whether the den meets in a leader's home, a church, or a school building, each den meeting has seven parts.

1. Before the meeting starts

2. While Cub Scouts gather

3. Opening

4. Business items

5. Activities

6. Closing

7. After the meeting

Now let's look at each part of the den meeting to see how you can help:

1. Before the Meeting Starts

You, the den leaders, and the denner arrive early. Be in full uniform or change into uniform after you arrive. Help the den leader and denner to

- Check equipment and supplies.
- Review who will handle the parts of the meeting.
- Set up the room.
- Prepare the songs, games, crafts, or other den meeting activities.

2. While the Cub Scouts Gather

- Greet the boys as they arrive.
- Show them where to put coats and school bags.
- Help boys with disabilities, if they need it.
- Check uniforming.
- Keep boys busy with a fun activity.
- Be ready with a game, trick, fitness exercise, or puzzle, or start each boy on a craft project or advancement.
- Give the denner and assistant denner a chance to help you.

3. Opening

Help the den leader to

- Get the boys to settle down. Use the Cub Scout sign for silence. Set a good example yourself.
- Lead the Pledge of Allegiance, the Cub Scout Promise, or a theme-related opening ceremony.
- Start off with a song or a yell or have a fun roll call. Use the theme of the month. For example, if the theme is nature, boys could respond with a bird call or by naming a tree or an animal.
- Help with a uniform inspection if the den leader asks. Don't embarrass any boy, but make suggestions if insignia are not worn properly. Be sure to set an example of proper uniforming yourself.

4. Business Items

Help the den leader to

- Collect dues.
- Check the boys' handbooks for advancement since the last meeting.
- Encourage and praise the Cub Scouts who have advanced and encourage those who are still working toward their next advancement.
- Explain the plans for the upcoming den and pack meetings.
- Serve and clean up refreshments if they are served in this part of the den meeting.

5. Activities

Help the den leader to

- Lead the planned activity. This may involve distributing supplies and materials for a craft or props for a skit. It will also mean and materials for a craft or props for a skit. It will also mean helping Cub Scouts do the project. They may take the project home to complete it there and then bring it back to the next den meeting or to the pack meeting.

- Teach the Cub Scouts a game or trick, or show them how to do some physical fitness exercises.
- Practice a skit for the pack meeting.
- Celebrate the birthday of a Cub Scout or den leader.
- Recognize Cub Scouts for completing achievements (Progress Toward Ranks beads).

6. Closing

Help the den leader to

- Get the boys to quiet down for the den leader's comments.
- Make announcements.
- Remind boys about the next meeting and what they must bring or be prepared to do.
- Lead or teach a boy to lead the closing ceremony. See page 93 for some ideas.
- See that boys are ready to go home and don't forget jackets, books, or school bags. Know whether each boy is allowed to walk home or whether he'll be picked up. Keep an eye on them if they are waiting outside.

7. After the Meeting

- Help the denner put the meeting place back in order.
- Review the meeting with den leaders.
- Make plans and assignments for next week's den meeting or the upcoming pack meeting. If you cannot attend a meeting or if you will be late, be sure to tell your den leader.

Encourage Advancement

Like you, Cub Scouts have badges and awards they can earn when they have passed the requirements. They can earn religious emblems also. In Cub Scouting, a boy's parent works with him and signs his book when he has done his best to do the requirements. (Webelos Scouts pass their requirements to their den leaders or activity badge counselors.)

There are five Cub Scout ranks:

1. Bobcat

2. Wolf

3. Bear

4. Webelos

5. Arrow of Light Award

Every new boy who joins the Cub Scouts first has to earn the Bobcat badge. What he has to do to earn it is in his *Wolf Cub Scout Book* or *Bear Cub Scout Book.*

If a boy is in second grade (or 8 years old), he works on his Wolf badge. His *Wolf Book* tells him everything he needs to do. If a boy is in the third grade (or 9 years old), he works on his Bear badge. Everything he needs to know is in his *Bear Book.* You should be familiar with both the *Wolf Book* and *Bear Book.*

Since you are working as a den chief to Cub Scouts, you will be involved with only three ranks: Bobcat, Wolf, and Bear.

Young boys like to know when they have done well. And they like to be told immediately. There are the immediate recognition beads they can earn as they work for their advancement ranks. This makes them feel good about how they are doing and encourages them. They also can earn arrow points.

A simple den ceremony should be held to recognize boys when they have earned advancements. Ranks and arrow points will be formally presented at pack meetings.

Help the Denner and Assistant Denner to Be Leaders

The denner and assistant denner are elected by the boys in the den to serve for a short period of time, usually a month. This helps to teach democracy. It is also the beginning of the experience you are familiar with, which is to have boys serve as leaders. Let the denners assist you and learn from you. Praise them for doing a good job.  Being a denner teaches them how to be a leader, and how to be a good follower, too.

You can help the denner be a leader by letting him help you. Show him how to do things, and then let him do them himself.

Encourage Cub Scouts to Become Webelos Scouts

As you work with the Cub Scout on his Bear badge, you can help him to feel so good about himself and his achievements that he will want to keep going. He will want to become a Webelos Scout when he is eligible. Point out to him the kinds of things Webelos Scouts do and the kinds of adventures they have. He can see this at pack meetings when the Webelos Scouts show off their skills.

The best encouragement Cub Scouts can have is to work with a den chief they like and admire—and that can be you! And you can remind them that the best way to become a Boy Scout is to prepare by becoming a Webelos Scout.

CHAPTER 4

The Webelos Den Chief

This section is for den chiefs to Webelos Scouts, who are in the fourth and fifth grades (or are 10 years old). In Chapters 1 and 2, you learned some general things about the Cub Scout program. In this chapter, you'll learn about working with Webelos Scouts. Webelos Scouts wear a different cap, neckerchief, and insignia. Webelos Scouts must earn the Bobcat badge if they did not earn it before in a Cub Scout den.

You have an important responsibility. You'll be giving these boys a taste of what it is like to be a Boy Scout. You can make a big difference. You can be the reason why a Webelos Scout chooses to become a Boy Scout. These boys are just one step away from Boy Scouting.

This might be a good time to go back and read again pages 20–21, which tell you what interests boys of this age have.

Duties of Webelos Den Chiefs

Here are some of the ways that you will be asked to help:

- Assist Webelos leaders as requested.

- Help with Webelos den meetings.

- Help Webelos Scouts earn activity badges, the Webelos badge, and the Arrow of Light Award.

- Know the Webelos activity badges that lead to Boy Scout advancement requirements.

- Help the Webelos denner and assistant denner to be leaders.

- Help with Webelos overnighters and other outdoor experiences.

- Help with joint Webelos Scout/Boy Scout activities.

- Keep in contact with the assistant Scoutmaster who is the Webelos resource person in your troop.

- Keep your troop leaders informed about pack activities and keep your den leaders informed about troop activities.

- Encourage Webelos Scouts to become Boy Scouts.

- Serve as recruiting officer for your troop, informing troop leaders about Webelos Scouts who are about to graduate.

- Help with the graduation ceremony when Webelos Scouts become Boy Scouts.

- Introduce Webelos Scouts into your troop.

Assist the Webelos Leader

Your Webelos leader may have an assistant. They are the leaders of a den of six to eight boys. Many of the boys will have been in a Cub Scout den, but some boys may be new to Cub Scouting.

The Webelos den usually meets once a week. The meeting may be early in the evening, on Saturday, or whenever convenient for the adult leaders. This den also attends pack meetings along with the other dens.

Your job as den chief is to help the leaders in the den meetings and at the pack meetings. You are the activities assistant. You may be asked to help the boys with their projects. You could also be involved in preparing for the den's part in the pack meeting. You'll learn more about that later. The important thing is to be an eager and willing helper. Don't wait to be asked. Look for ways in which you can offer your help and leadership.

Your Webelos den leader may be new. You may know more about Webelos Scouting than he or she does. So, you can be a big help and resource. You are on the same team, and you have an opportunity to be a team player with the leaders.

The Den Meeting

The den meeting may be in a leader's home or in a building that is convenient for those who belong to the pack.

The Webelos Scout den meeting has seven parts:

1. Before the meeting starts

2. Gathering

3. Opening

4. Activity badge fun

5. Preparation

6. Closing

7. After the meeting

Let's look at each part of the den meeting to see where you fit in.

1. Before the Meeting Starts

You, the Webelos den leaders, and the denner arrive early. Be in full uniform or change into your uniform after you arrive. Help the Webelos den leader and denner to

- Check equipment and supplies.
- Review who will handle the parts of the meeting.
- Set up the room.
- Prepare the songs, games, and other den meeting activities.

2. Gathering

- Greet the boys as they arrive.
- Show them where to put coats and school bags.
- Help Cub Scouts with disabilities, if they need it.
- If asked, help by checking attendance, collecting dues, or inspecting uniforms. Don't embarrass any boy, but make suggestions if insignia are not worn properly. Be sure to set an example of proper uniforming yourself.
- Keep the boys busy with a fun activity. This could be a game, trick, fitness exercise, or puzzle.

3. Opening

Help the Webelos leader to

- Lead the Pledge of Allegiance, the Cub Scout Promise, the Boy Scout Oath or Law, or a theme-related opening ceremony.
- Start off with a song or yell or have a fun roll call.

4. Activity Badge Fun

- Help the boys with their activity badge work.
- Be familiar with the requirements for the activity badge for this meeting.
- See that the boys are having fun. The den meeting shouldn't be like sitting in a classroom.
- Be ready to teach the boys a skill you have learned as a Boy Scout.
- Point out the activity badge requirements that lead to Boy Scout advancement requirements.

5. Preparation

- Assist or guide the boys in this "action" time. Equipment or props may have to be built for an outdoor experience or for the pack meeting.

- Encourage the boys to suggest things they want to do or places they want to go. Help make plans.
- Tell them about Boy Scout activities that they can participate in, such as a Scouting show.

6. Closing
- Help in making announcements.
- Be involved in the closing ceremony. See page 93 of this book for ideas on closing ceremonies, or use the *Boy Scout Handbook*.

7. After the Meeting
- Help the denner get the meeting place back in order.
- Review the meeting with the Webelos den leaders.
- Make plans and assignments for next week's den meeting or the upcoming pack meeting.

The Pack Meeting

You have just read about the parts of a Webelos den meeting. There is another important meeting of which you will be a part. This is the pack meeting. Your den will have a part or an assignment in that meeting. Your den may have to prepare a display table of the things they have been working on all month. They could be asked to do a ceremony or demonstrate a Scouting skill.

Other ways you may be asked to assist at pack meetings are to arrive early and help get the place ready. Or you could be asked to seat the parents and families. Help your Webelos Scouts behave well and encourage them to do their part in the meeting.

Help Webelos Scouts Advance

Because one of the goals of the Webelos den is to prepare boys to become Boy Scouts, Webelos activities and the advancement plan are quite similar to yours as a Scout.

You should be familiar with the *Webelos Scout Book*. The book describes the 20 activity badges the boys work on. The activities of each den meeting are usually aimed at one of these activity badges. Activity badge areas are like your merit badges. Here are the subjects, arranged by their activity badge groups:

Physical Skills

Aquanaut
Athlete
Fitness
Sportsman

Mental Skills

Artist
Scholar
Showman
Traveler

Community

Citizen
Communicator
Family Member
Readyman

Technology

Craftsman
Engineer
Handyman
Scientist

Outdoor

Forester
Geologist
Naturalist
Outdoorsman

If you have earned a merit badge in one of these topics, you'll be a great help to your Webelos Scouts as they work on that activity badge.

The den leader may call in activity badge counselors to help the boys on some of these badges.

All Webelos Scouts should earn the Webelos badge. After that, they can receive the compass points emblem by earning four more activity badges. They may receive a compass point for their badge for every four additional activity badges. They should go on to earn the highest award in Cub Scouting, the Arrow of Light Award. The boy who earns this award will be able to move easily into Boy Scouting. This is one of your purposes as a den chief.

And that's not all; there is also a religious emblems program. A Webelos Scout may want to earn one of these important emblems. Encourage him to do so.

You also may have a part in a ceremony at the pack meeting where your boys will receive their advancement badges.

Help the Webelos Denner and Assistant Denner Learn to Be Leaders

The denner and assistant denner are elected by the boys in the den to serve for a few months. This process helps to teach democracy. It is also the beginning of the experience you are familiar with and that is to have boys your own age as your leaders. Let the denners assist you and learn from you. Praise them for a job well done.

Help With Outdoor Activities

Some Webelos Scouts may have a lot of experience in outdoor activities and camping. Others may have very little. As Webelos Scouts, they will have additional opportunities to go camping with a parent. These will be as a Webelos den, and perhaps as a part of a campout with a Boy Scout troop.

You can help prepare the Webelos Scouts for the fun of camping by telling them about your experiences. Help them plan what to take in order to be prepared for the weather as well as the program that is planned. Your experience in camping in various places in all kinds of weather will help them learn that even rain can't dampen the fun of a campout.

Your Webelos den may also go on hiking trips, attend sports events, or take part in district or council Cub Scout activities. You will be able to help with the planning of all of these exciting events.

Help With Joint Pack/Troop Activities

One sure way to help your boys move easily into Boy Scouting is to give them a taste of what happens in a troop. You can help. Plan for your troop to host a joint meeting with your Webelos Scouts. This might be a court of honor or other special activity. Your troop can invite the Webelos den and parents to go on overnight campouts. Use your imagination and think of things that Webelos Scouts would find exciting about Boy Scouting.

Ask to be invited to the meeting of the patrol leaders' council, which will be planning the joint activity. Help with the planning. Tell them about your Webelos Scouts and the activity badges they are working on.

Keep in Contact With the Assistant Scoutmaster

Each troop should have an assistant Scoutmaster whose job is to keep good communications between the troop and the Webelos den. This person may arrange for the den to visit troop meetings and activities or to use the troop's camping equipment.

The assistant Scoutmaster may also help to get counselors for Webelos activity badges and to tell the parents of your Webelos Scouts about Boy Scouting. This troop resource person may be one of the people who will train you to be a Webelos den chief.

Keep Your Troop Leaders Informed

You can be the communications person between your den and your troop. This part of your job is to let your troop leaders know what you are doing for the den and the pack. If you need help from your troop, ask for it.

If the pack is putting on an event or doing a community service, be sure to tell your troop. They might like to help or they might come to see what your boys are doing.

You will represent the Webelos den as a part of the patrol leaders' council when joint activities of the troop and Webelos den are planned.

Encourage Webelos Scouts to Become Boy Scouts

By your example, you are already encouraging Webelos Scouts to become Boy Scouts. Because you cared enough to become a den chief, you are the best encouragement for the Webelos Scouts to want to become Boy Scouts.

But you can do more. Talk with them. Tell them about the adventures, the hiking, the camping, the learning to make yourself comfortable while living in the outdoors. Tell them about the fun you have. Let them know about the good friends you have made.

If Scouting has helped you in your school work, tell them. Maybe now you have a hobby or even a career in mind that you didn't have before you became a Boy Scout. Tell them how Scouting got you interested.

This is the easiest part of your job as a den chief. It's easy to sell someone on an idea that you believe in and have fun with.

You know the good feeling you get when you are presented with a badge or a troop honor. If it is given to you by your leaders in front of the troop and your family, you feel even more proud. Your Webelos Scouts need to be praised and encouraged, too.

Webelos Scouts who earn the Arrow of Light Award and are ready for Boy Scouting should have an especially fine ceremony. You can help to make that happen. The book *Cub Scout Ceremonies for Dens and Packs* contains some good ideas. Find out whether your pack has a copy.

Be a Recruiting Officer

If you have done your job well as a den chief, you should have six or eight boys eager to become Boy Scouts in your troop or some other troop. This is a natural for you. You've set the example. You've been a good den chief. You know your boys. So, now all you have to do is to tell your troop leaders about your boys.

Help arrange for visits to your troop. If there are several troops in the area, some Webelos Scouts may want to visit another troop. This is all right. The important thing is that every one of the Webelos Scouts has a chance to join a troop. Don't give up until they have all had the opportunity to select a troop and be welcomed into Boy Scouting.

But sometimes even with the best den chief and den leader, one or two Webelos Scouts will not join a troop. If you have done your best, don't feel bad if not everyone joins. Either way, your Webelos Scouts always will remember you and what you did for them. You've done a tremendously important Good Turn for Scouting and for yourself. Congratulations!

CHAPTER 5

Den Chief Ideas Chest

This "Ideas Chest" will give you plenty of things to do for gathering-time activities as well as games, songs, and other ideas to keep Cub Scouts active and busy. The Ideas Chest sections are:

- Tricks and Puzzles

- Songs

- Homemade Games

- Indoor Games

- Outdoor Games

- Fitness Games

- Skits, Puppets, and Pantomimes

- Ceremonies

Leading the den members in games, songs, tricks, contests, and other activities is one of your most important jobs. Make sure you know and practice the instructions for leading the activity and have all equipment ready before starting. Be sure that you understand the steps to follow:

1. Choose an activity that fits the place, the number of boys, the time available, and the type of den meeting.

2. Prepare by choosing the equipment needed for the activity and by having it ready.

3. Practice before the den meeting.

4. Explain the activity to the den members clearly and briefly.

5. Always use the Cub Scout sign as a signal for getting attention.

Tricks and Puzzles

Tricks and puzzles will help liven up the gathering time part of your den meetings. Cub Scouts enjoy trying to solve a trick or puzzle, learning new ones, or simply outdoing their buddies.

As den chief, you can take charge of these fun-filled activities. The denner can help lead them. Your den leader will give you ideas, and *The Cub*

Scout Leader How-To Book has many more ideas. Ask your den leader whether you can borrow a copy so you can learn more tricks and puzzles.

Come to each den meeting prepared to show the boys a new trick or stunt. These activities will help keep the den meeting moving and the members busy doing something they enjoy.

BLOCK PUZZLES. These simple puzzles can be fun to make and use. Have boys draw a puzzle design on light cardboard and separate into pieces as shown. Jumble the pieces and see who can assemble his puzzle first.

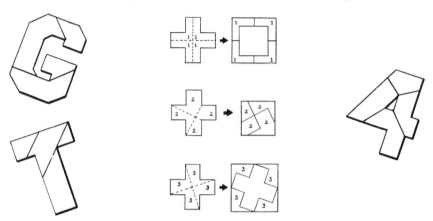

WHIMMY DIDDLE. You can use this trick to amaze your den. Fasten a light propeller to the end of a notched stick or dowel with a pin or nail. By rubbing the notched edge of the stick, you can make the propeller revolve. At will, you can stop the propeller and reverse the direction of its revolution.

Do this trick by rubbing a pencil along the nicked edge of the stick to set up vibrations that will cause the propeller to revolve rapidly. The direction of the revolution can be controlled by light pressure with the thumb or forefinger on one side of the notched stick or the other. Do this without being observed and credit the change of direction to your will power.

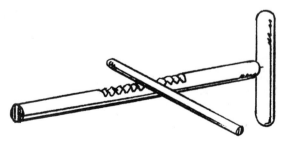

BUTTONHOLER. Make a buttonholer from a tongue depressor or craft stick with a loop of string through a hole in one end of it. The string must be shorter than the stick. Have boys loop string through the buttonhole in another Cub Scout's shirt pocket. The trick is to remove it without untying the string.

To attach the buttonholer to the shirt, pull the pocket flap through the loop of the string until the point of the stick can be inserted in the buttonhole and the string drawn up tight. It is impossible to remove the stick in the usual way, because the string is shorter than the stick. Show boys how they can remove it by pulling the string back over the pocket flap and withdrawing the stick, eye first.

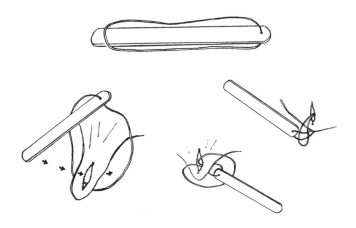

MAGIC KNOT. Get several pieces of string about 2 feet long to teach Cub Scouts the magic overhand knot. It is done by tying an overhand knot in the middle of a string without letting go of either end. First, let

the Cub Scouts try it, and then show them the trick. Put the string on the floor or table. Fold your arms as illustrated, stoop, and pick up the ends of the string. While rising, uncross your arms but keep your hold on the string, and presto!—the overhand knot will appear.

LIFT A BOTTLE. You can lift a bottle with a soda straw if first you bend the straw as shown. Push it into the bottle and lift up slowly.

SECRET CODES. Cub Scouts can have fun and complete a requirement for Wolf Elective 1, "It's a Secret," by making up their own den code and sending secret messages.

Cub Scouts enjoy making up secret codes and other ways of signaling. Help the boys in your den invent their own code. When you are ready to help them work out a code, talk the idea over first with your den leader and plan a code game to help boys learn and have fun at the same time.

Try a simple code like this:

Xf xjmm hp

Suppose you want to send the message, "We will go." Have your boys make up a coded message by substituting the next letter of the alphabet for the actual ones in the words of the message. For example: "We" becomes "Xf." "Will" would be "xjmm." The entire message would read "Xf xjmm hp."

Try substituting numbers, marks, lines, boxes, etc., for letters. Let den members dream on this project.

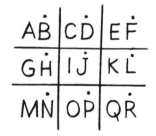

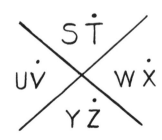

Plan games around the codes. Using the scheme **shown above,** the message "We will go," becomes—

< L   < □ Ｌ   Ｌ   ⊐ ⊓

The boys will soon catch on and try a few of their own.

These codes, plus the suggestions in the *Wolf Cub Scout Book,* will give you plenty of ideas for secret code games.

SNATCH THE COIN. This is a test of skill and alertness. One Cub Scout holds a small coin in his outstretched palm. Another holds his hand, palm down, about 12 inches above the coin. He tries to snatch the coin before the holder can close his hand. He can do it, too. The trick is for the snatcher to strike the other fellow's palm smartly with his fingertips. This throws the coin up into the snatcher's hand. The holder must hold his hand wide open until he sees the snatcher's hand go down.

BEHIND YOUR BACK. With your hands behind your back and away from the audience, loop a piece of rope about 18 inches long around one wrist and cross the ends. Place your other wrist, with your hand pointing in the opposite direction, over this crossed rope and ask someone to tie the two rope ends tightly over your hand. Turn around to show that you are tied. Then face the audience again. Twist your hands around to point in the same direction, and you will have a large loop through which you can easily draw out one hand and show it to your amazed audience.

To complete the trick, put your hand back through the loop, twist your hands in opposite directions, and ask doubters to inspect the knot.

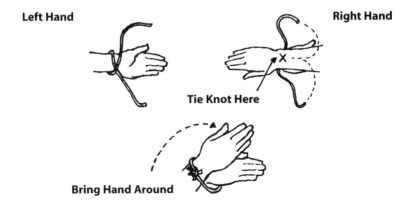

Left Hand

Right Hand

Tie Knot Here

Bring Hand Around

PRISONER'S ESCAPE. Tie a piece of string around the wrists of one of the boys in your den. Loop another piece of string over his wrist and tie it to the wrists of a second Cub Scout. They are now locked together. Challenge them to get away without breaking the string or untying a knot. When they give up, show them how. Push the center of the string of one Cub Scout through the loop on the inside of the other's wrist, bring this new loop back over his hand, and draw it back through the wrist loop. They will be free. See the diagram for help on doing this trick.

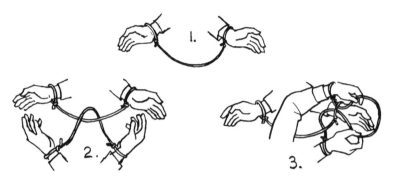

MAGIC PICKUP. Drop five toothpicks on a table. Be sure they are not in an even row. Pick them up as follows:

First toothpick between your two thumbs; second one between your two first fingers; third one between your two second fingers; fourth one between your two third fingers; and fifth one between your two little fingers.

You must lift toothpicks lengthwise to complete the trick. Neat trick if you can do it!

YOKE PUZZLE. Make this puzzle from a 1-by 6-inch piece of thin board (a tongue depressor or craft stick is excellent), string, and two washers. Bore holes in the board and fasten the string and washers as shown.

Challenge the boys to get the washers together without untying any of the knots.

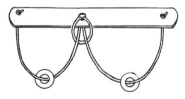

Show them how to do it. Have them pull the loop at the center hole straight out about 2 inches. Slide the washer through the loop, and then pull the rest of the center loop back through the center hole. Slide the washer through the center loop onto the opposite loop. Pull the center loop back through the hole. The washer is now hanging on the opposite loop. Reverse the procedure to get it back.

STRAP AND BUTTON PUZZLE. Make two parallel cuts in the center of a strip of firm, pliable leather or vinyl. Just below this, cut a hole the same width. Then pass a heavy string under the slit and through the hole, as illustrated. Fasten buttons to the loose ends of the string.

The object is to remove the string without taking off the buttons. Boys can do this by bending the leather and drawing the narrow strip through the hole. The string and buttons then can be removed easily.

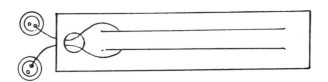

IMPOSSIBLE. This looks easy, but it can't be done. Place both heels squarely against the wall and then try to pick something up from the floor and straighten up again without moving your feet.

FRANKFURTER. Hold your two index fingers at eye level a little apart. Keep your eyes on the center but look into the distance; you'll see a magic frankfurter floating between your fingers.

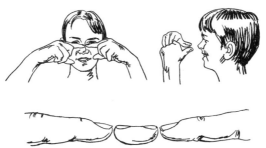

HIDDEN TOOTHPICK. Amaze your den with this trick. Secretly put a toothpick in a hem of a handkerchief before demonstrating this trick. Ask a Cub Scout to place a second toothpick in the handkerchief and fold it several times. Let one of the boys feel the toothpick in the hem and ask him to break it in two or three pieces. Make a few magic motions over the handkerchief, unfold it, and remove the second toothpick without a single break. Teach the trick and ask Cub Scouts to try it on their parents.

HAND HYPNOSIS. Cub Scouts will enjoy mystifying friends with this stunt. Have a boy stroke the palms of another's hands several times. After making a false stroking motion, he should stop suddenly—and the other boy's hands will rise mysteriously.

JUMP TWO. Challenge the members of your den to take 10 objects—coins, matches, pebbles, or washers—and jump each one over two others to form five piles of twos.

Drive 10 brads into a small strip of wood at 1-inch intervals and place a washer over each brad to make a convenient puzzle. Number each brad.

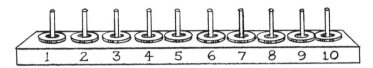

Solve the puzzle by moving washers as follows: 5 to 2, 7 to 10, 3 to 8, 1 to 4, and 9 to 6.

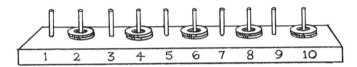

Stretch a rubber band along the tops of the washers to keep them from being lost when you're not using the puzzle.

THREE-IN-A-ROW. Put three coins in a row on a table. The puzzle is to see whether you can remove the middle coin from the center without touching it.

Solution: Move the coin at the left over to the right end of the row. This changes the position of the original middle coin, putting it at the left end of the row.

STRONG MAN. Place your palm on top of your head. Then ask a Cub Scout to take hold of your wrist and lift your hand off your head. It can't be done if you hold your hand firmly in place.

THE EXPANDING HOLE. In the center of a piece of paper, cut a round hole about the size of a dime. Give this paper and a quarter to a Cub Scout and ask him to try to pass the quarter through the hole without tearing the paper or touching the coin. When he fails, take the paper back. Fold it in half so the fold is across the hole. Have someone slip the quarter in between the folds. Hold the extreme ends of the paper where the fold is. Raise them upward and toward each other. Shake the paper gently, and the quarter will slip through the hole.

MAGIC STRAW. Cut a slit in the middle of a straw. Thread a string through the straw. Tell the Cub Scouts you can cut the straw in half without cutting the string.

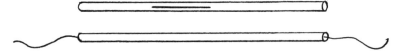

Solution: Bend the straw. Pull the string out of the slit, and then cut the straw.

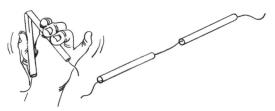

MAGNETIC SPOON. Rub a spoon, pretending to magnetize it. Hold the spoon as shown. Show to audience. The spoon seems to stick to your hand.

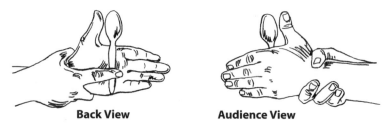

Back View   **Audience View**

BOTTOMS UP. Stand three plastic tumblers in a row with the middle one upside down. With three moves, picking up only two and turning them over with each move, end up with all three "bottoms up" in the three moves.

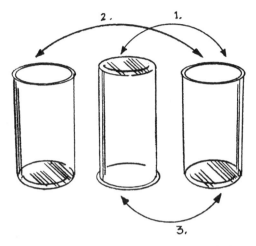

Solution: First move—turn over second and third tumblers. Second move—turn over first and third. Third move—turn over second and third again.

For more ideas ask a leader to help you find *Group Meeting Sparklers, Cub Scout Program Helps,* the *Webelos Leader Guide,* the *Cub Scout Fun Book,* and the *Cub Scout Leader How-to-Book.*

Songs

(See page 14 for tips on leading songs.)

THINGS TO DO WITH SONGS

1. Add motions that will fit the words.

2. Leave words out and use handclaps instead of the words. For example: "The More We Get Together"—clap every time the word "together" should be sung.

3. Add musical instruments or rhythm instruments.

4. If you or a den member plays an instrument, use it to accompany the songs.

SOAP, SOAP, SOAP AND TOWEL
(*Tune:* "Row, Row, Row Your Boat")

Soap, soap, soap, and towel
Towel and water, please
Merrily, merrily, merrily, merrily
Scrub your dirty knees.

BANANAS, COCONUTS, GRAPES
(*Tune:* "Battle Hymn of the Republic")

I like bananas, coconuts, and grapes,
I like bananas, coconuts, and grapes,
I like bananas, coconuts, and grapes,
That's why they call me
(*Yell*) Tarzan of the Apes!

HORSE FLY
(*Tune:* "The More We Get Together")

Did you ever see a horse fly, a horse fly, a horse fly?
Did you ever see a horse fly, a horse fly, fly, fly?
Did you ever see a board walk, a board walk, a board walk?
Did you ever see a board walk, a board walk, walk, walk?
(*Variations:* Shoe lace, hair pin, tooth pick, eye drop, neck tie, eye lash, yard stick, ear drum)

CUB SCOUT MARCHING SONG
(*Tune:* "The Children's Marching Song")

This Cub Scout, number one,
He just likes to get things done.

Chorus (Repeat after each stanza.)

With a knick knack paddy wack
Give Cub Scouts a chore;
This they'll do and ask for more.

This Cub Scout, number two,
He will do odd jobs for you.

This Cub Scout, number three,
Is full of humor, full of glee.

This Cub Scout, number four,
Follows rules and knows the score.

This Cub Scout, number five,
He has courage, he has drive.

This Cub Scout, number six,
He makes things with ropes and sticks.

This Cub Scout, number seven,
He was sent to us from heaven.

This Cub Scout, number eight,
Gives goodwill and sure does rate.

This Cub Scout, number nine,
He is pleasant all the time.

This Cub Scout, number 10,
Sings the chorus once again.

FOUND A PEANUT
(*Tune:* "Clementine")

Found a peanut, found a peanut,
Found a peanut last night,
Last night I found a peanut,
Found a peanut last night.

2. It was rotten.
3. Ate it anyway.
4. Got a stomachache.
5. Called the doctor.
6. Got some medicine.
7. Died anyway.
8. Went to heaven.
9. Met Saint Peter.
10. I was hungry.
11. He gave me a peanut.

BINGO
There was a farmer had a dog,
And Bingo was his name-o:
B-I-N-G-O, B-I-N-G-O, B-I-N-G-O
And Bingo was his name-o.

(Sing the song through six times, the first time spelling out the name B-I-N-G-O; the second time, spelling out the first four letters and clapping the *O*; the third time, spelling out the first three letters and clapping the *G* and *O;* and so on, until all five letters are clapped out.)

THERE WERE THREE JOLLY FISHERMEN

There were three jolly fishermen,
There were three jolly fishermen,
(Group 1 shouts:) "Fisher, fisher"
(Group 2 shouts:) "Men, men, men"
(Group 1 shouts:) "Fisher, fisher"
(Group 2 shouts:) "Men, men, men"
There were three jolly fishermen.

The first one's name was Abraham,
The first one's name was Abraham,
Abra, Abra; ham, ham, ham, *etc.*

The second one's name was I-I-saac,
The second one's name was I-I-saac,
I-I, I-I; zik, zik, zik, *etc.*

The third one's name was Ja-a-cob,
The third one's name was Ja-a-cob,
Ja-a, Ja-a; cob, cob, cob, *etc.*

They all went up to Jericho,
They all went up to Jericho,
Jer-i, Jer-i; cho, cho, cho, *etc.*

They should have gone to Amsterdam,
They should have gone to Amsterdam,
Amster, Amster, shh, shh, shh, *etc.*

THE BEAR SONG

The other day *(the other day),*
I met a bear *(I met a bear)*
Out in the woods *(out in the woods)*
Away out there *(away out there).*

The other day,
I met a bear
out in the woods
away out there.

He looked at me,
I looked at him.
He sized up me,
I sized up him.

He said to me,
"Why don't you run?"
I see you ain't
Got any gun."

And so I ran
Away from there,
And right behind
Me was the bear.

And then I see
Ahead of me
A great big tree—
O glory be!

The lowest branch
Was 10 feet up.
I'd have to jump
And trust my luck.

And so I jumped
Into the air.
I missed that branch
Away up there.

Now don't you fret,
And don't you frown,
I caught that branch
On the way back down.

That's all there is,
There ain't no more,
Unless I see
That bear once more.

For more songs, see the *Cub Scout Songbook* and the *Boy Scout Songbook.*

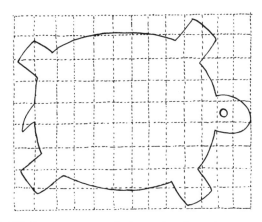

TURTLE RACE. Boys can cut their turtles from heavy cardboard, plywood, or floor tile using scissors, a jigsaw, or a coping saw. They will enjoy decorating their turtles.

Race the turtles on heavy cords 20 feet long. Fasten one end to a support the same height as the hole in the turtle. To begin the race, hold the cords taut, with the turtles leaning slightly toward the "jockeys" (the boys) On the signal "go," race the turtles toward the jockeys by tightening and relaxing the cords so that the turtles move along slowly in turtle fashion. The first turtle to touch the finish line wins.

RING TOSS. Make five rings out of rope, rubber, heavy cardboard, or stiff wire, or use rubber fruit-jar rings or lids from yogurt or cottage cheese containers with the centers cut out. Let each player toss rings in turn at a stick driven into the ground or set in a stand for indoor use. Each ringer counts three points; leaner, two; nearest to stick, one.

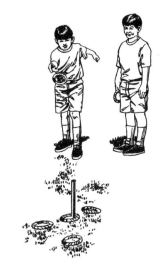

PIE TIN WASHER TOSS. Let each player toss five washers at a pie tin. Score one point for each washer that remains in the tin.

RING THE BOTTLE. Provide several soda bottles, rings, string, and sticks for this game. One way to play is to try to place the ring over the neck of the bottle. When you can do this, lay the bottle on its side and attempt to pull it upright with the ring and string.

ZUNI RING GAME. You will need a stick, string, and rings. Tie one end of the string to the stick and the other end to a ring. The object is to swing the ring forward and catch it on the end of the stick. The Zunis twisted a twig into a circle and tied it with blue yarn to make the ring, but you can use a rubber ring seal from a canning jar or something similar. Some Zuni ring games have three or more rings; a player who rings a small ring scores four points, but only two for the larger rings.

BEANBAG TOSS. Make the target by painting a face on plywood and cutting openings for the eyes and mouth. Each boy in turn tosses five beanbags, scoring three points for hitting the eyes and one point for the mouth.

SODA BOTTLE BOWLING. Collect 10 empty plastic soda bottles with lids (or dishwashing liquid containers). You may want to add a little sand to the bottoms for stability. Line the bottles up as in bowling. Draw a line about 20 feet back from the bottles. Each Cub Scout is given two bean bags to throw underhanded at the bottles as in regular bowling. Keep score by counting the number of "pins" knocked down.

This can also be played relay fashion. Each Cub Scout sets up the pins for the next boy in line after he completes his toss. Each team receives points for the total number of pins knocked down. This is not a speed race.

BOX HOCKEY. To start the game, two players stand on opposite sides of the hockey box. After crossing their sticks three times, they put the puck into play from the top of the partition separating the two courts. Each player tries to play the puck toward the outside hole, on his opponent's side of the box. A point is scored each time a player knocks the puck through the outside hole.

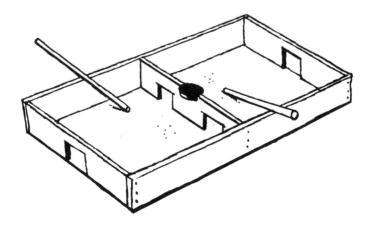

BOUNCEBALL. The idea of this simple game is to bounce a rubber ball into a target on the first bounce. Use a wastebasket, paper bag, or box for a target. Each time a player lands a ball in the target, he gets a point. Vary the game by using several balls of different colors and counting different scores for each.

BOWL AND BOUNCE. Each Cub Scout, in turn, rolls a ball up the incline so that it falls through one of the numbered holes. Give each boy three chances and score according to the numbers.

CAN THE CAN. Select four or five tin cans that nest into one another and set them in a row. Make a stick on a string as illustrated. The stick should be a little longer than the largest can is wide and should be sharp so that it hooks on the inside edge of the can. The string should be tied on the stick a little off center so that one end of the stick is higher than the other when the string is being held.

The object of the game is to tip the high end of the stick down into the second can; if you are careful, the stick will wedge on the side lip of the can so you can lift the can into the next larger one. Continue this until all cans are nested.

You can find more ideas for homemade games in the *Cub Scout Leader How-To Book, Cub Scout Fun Book,* and *Cub Scout Program Helps.*

Indoor Games

GLIDERS. Hold a glider contest using paper gliders. Try for distance and accuracy. Land the glider in a target area such as a wastebasket.

ZIP-ZAP. This is a good game for indoors and for den meetings in small quarters.

Form a circle with one boy in the center. The boy in the center points to one of the other boys in the circle and says either "zip" or "zap" and counts to five. If the player in the center says "zip," the player pointed at must give the name of the player on his right before the count is up. If the player in the center says "zap," the player pointed at must give the name of the player to the left.

BIRD, BEAST, OR FISH. Players all sit in circle except one, who is "It." He points or throws a knotted handkerchief to some player and calls out "beast" or "bird" or "fish" and quickly counts to 10. If the player has not named whatever was called in that time, he becomes "It." No one may use the name of any bird, beast, or fish that another has already named until "It" changes.

KIM'S GAME. Arrange 20 different objects in an orderly way on a tray or table. Cover the objects with a sheet of newspaper until the game begins, when you'll lift the sheet and let the Cub Scouts study the objects silently for one or two minutes. Then replace the cover. The Cub Scouts move to another part of the room and individually write down the names of all of the objects they can remember. The one with the longest correct list wins.

The objects can be related to the theme of the month, such as nature objects for a nature theme.

TOUCH AND TELL. Have the members of your den stand shoulder to shoulder in a circle, facing in, with their hands behind them and their eyes closed. Pass a number of small objects, one at a time, to the denner. He feels each one and passes it on to the player on his right, who does the same. When the objects have completely passed around the circle, ask each player to tell one of the items he was able to identify and remember. Go around the circle until all of the objects have been identified.

FIND THE LEADER. The Cub Scouts sit in a circle. Select one to be "It" and have him leave the room. The remaining Cub Scouts select a leader. The leader begins an action, such as clapping. "It" is then called back into the center of the circle. The leader slyly changes the motion, such as making a face, snapping fingers, patting his head, etc. The others in the circle immediately imitate the leader. "It" watches everyone to try to determine who is leading the motions. The leader should change motions frequently. When "It" discovers who the leader is, the leader becomes the new "It" and the game starts over. Give "It" four or five chances to identify the leader. If he is unsuccessful, congratulate the leader and have him become the new "It."

CALENDAR PITCH. Place one page from a large desk calendar on the floor as the target. Each Cub Scout tosses three checkers or bottle caps from a distance of 5 or 6 feet, and totals his score according to the numbers on which his markers land. Markers on a line don't count. The winning score might be 75 points or more. For added excitement, score double points for holidays, such as eight points for Independence Day (July 4th).

NAIL-DRIVING CONTEST. This game will help Cub Scouts develop their wrists and arms and improve their coordination and accuracy.

Divide the den into two teams. Line up the teams for a relay race about 10 feet from the driving area. Provide each team with a piece of two-by-four about 1 foot long, a hammer, and nails shorter than the thickness of the wood. Each boy runs to the board, drives two nails, runs back, and gives the hammer to the next player. The team driving the most nails straight wins.

Have boys switch hands for a variation of this contest.

KNOT-TYING CONTESTS. Cub Scouts enjoy rope and knot games. They know knot tying is a part of Boy Scout advancement requirements as well.

Before you teach any knot game, be sure every Cub Scout can tie the knot used in that game. Here are some tips on teaching knots:

As part of your den equipment, have a 3-foot length of sash cord for each member. Whip the ends so they won't fray. (This is part of Bear Achievement 22.)

When teaching Cub Scouts to tie a knot, stand with your back toward them. Raise your hands and the rope so they can see them clearly in the same way that you do. Don't talk about right hand and left hand. Just let them tie the knot with you, step by step. Don't expect that all Cub Scouts will get the knot the first time. Tie each knot at least three times. Give individual help to boys who need it.

Invite the knot-tying champion of your troop or patrol to visit your den when you are playing.

SHOESTRING RELAY. This game will help Cub Scouts complete the requirements for Wolf Elective 17, "Tie It Right."

First, teach them to tie a square bow knot, the correct shoestring tie. Divide the den into two teams and give each team time to practice. If there is an odd number of boys, use the denner as a judge. In relay fashion, one team runs to the den leader and the other to the den chief. When he reaches the leader, each boy ties his shoestring and runs back to touch off the next player. Score one point for each correct tie and one extra point for the team that is first to tie a given number of correct knots.

SQUARE KNOT PULLOVER. Divide players into two teams and line them up facing each other, with a line down the middle separating the two teams. Each player passes his rope around his own waist and lets his opponent hold the ends. Now you can start the game. At the starting signal, each player, without any interference from his opponent, ties a square knot in the ends of the rope around his opponent's waist. The instant he finishes the knot, he pulls on the rope and tries to pull his opponent over the line.

Caution: This game will not succeed if the Cub Scouts don't stick to the rule about not interfering with each other while tying the knots. Also caution them to pull on the ropes only, not uniforms.

CIRCLE KNOT RACE. Explain the game and show how to tie a square knot or sheet bend (used for joining ropes).

Divide the Cub Scouts into two teams and have each team form a circle. At the word "go," each boy grabs the end of the rope of the player to his right, joins his rope to it, and steps into the circle. The team that is first to have all its players standing inside the circle with correct knots wins.

Note: It isn't necessary to tell you that boys like to cheer. Why not let them give their den cheer when all members are in the circle. That will make it easier for you to judge the winner.

Outdoor Games

HAND BADMINTON. To prepare for this simple home game, first show boys how to make their own "popouts," as shown and described below. The object of the game is to keep the popout off the ground. Play boy against boy or one-half of the den against the other half. Use a rope, a line on the ground, or a net to mark off a center line that the popout must cross in flight.

Make sure that the popout is packed firmly so it will travel faster. Each time a team allows the popout to touch the ground, score one point against it.

1. Insert feather in three holes punched in cardboard circle.

2. Bend quills over and tape down.

3. Stuff toe of old sock with cotton. Put feather base inside and secure with rubber band or string.

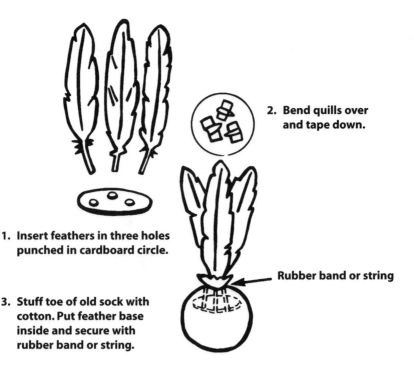

2. **Bend quills over and tape down.**

1. **Insert feathers in three holes punched in cardboard circle.**

Rubber band or string

3. **Stuff toe of old sock with cotton. Put feather base inside and secure with rubber band or string.**

ROPE-THROWING CONTEST. This is an excellent game to play while Cub Scouts are arriving at a den meeting. Let the denner start it as soon as the first Cub Scouts arrive. This game will help the Cub Scouts with Bear Achievement 22, "Tying It All Up," and will help Webelos Scouts earn the Aquanaut activity badge.

Before beginning, do four things:

1. Get a long piece of rope or join short pieces to make a single line. Tie a small stick or other weight to the end of the line.

2. Show Cub Scouts how to coil and throw a rope. Have a right-handed Cub Scout coil the rope in his right hand and a left-handed Cub Scout in his left hand.

3. Make a target by drawing three circles—one within the other, 1-, 2-, and 3-feet in diameter—on the floor or on the ground.

4. Have a paper and pencil ready for keeping score.

Let each player have three tries coiling and throwing the rope at the target. If any part of the rope is touching the small circle, score three points; score two points for the second circle and one for the outer circle.

TIE AND JUMP. This game will help Cub Scouts learn skills to pass the requirements for Wolf Elective 17, "Tie It Right." Begin by teaching a simple knot. Make sure every player can tie it. Practice the standing long jump.

Line up the players side by side. At the word "go," they all start tying the knot. On the command "Drop ropes!" everyone drops his rope in front of him. Have every player who correctly ties his knot pick up his rope and stand with his toes on the long jump starting line. After you (or other den leaders) have completed inspecting the knot, conduct the standing long jump.

Using the jumping area as the new starting point, repeat the game two, three, or more times, depending on the space you have for jumping. The Cub Scout who jumps the greatest distance is the winner.

CATCH-AND-THROW RACE. Form two teams and line them up in relay formation. Select one player on each team to act as "starter." Station each starter about 35 feet in front of his team.

At the word "go," each starter throws his ball to the player at the head of his team. This player catches the ball, throws it back to the starter, and then gets out of the way by sitting or squatting. Each player in turn catches the ball, throws it back, and sits or squats. In case of fumbles, the player must chase the ball and throw it after returning to his place in line.

Make up your own rules for this game. Don't worry if the teams are uneven in number, as the team that completes a certain number of throws first wins.

If you arrange the game so each player must catch and throw several times, all those who succeed will have completed part of the requirements for Wolf Achievement 1, "Feats of Skill."

NATURE HUNT. Try this game the next time your den goes on an outing or whenever you work on a nature theme.

Ask your den leader to help you make up a list of nature objects your den can search for. Here are a few ideas, but you'll have many more of your own:

- An oak leaf
- A seed of any type (Be careful of the den leader's garden!)
- A clover leaf (four-leaf clover, if one can be found)
- A berry
- An acorn

Tell the Cub Scouts that they may pick up objects on the ground, but may not pick leaves or seeds from trees or bushes.

In starting the hunt, you should name only the first object to be found. As soon as a Cub Scout finds the first object, he should bring it to you and you can give him the name of the next one. The first boy to find all objects wins.

RUNNING LONG JUMP. This game gives the less-experienced jumpers just as important a part as the better jumpers.

Divide the den into two teams, and let the captains coach their teams. The first contestant on each team toes the starting line and takes a running long jump. The second member starts his running jump where the first member of his team finished, and so on. The team that has its members out in front after an equal number of jumps wins.

Fitness Games

ROOSTER FIGHT. Two Cub Scouts stand in a circle 6 feet in diameter. Each holds his left foot with his right hand behind his back, and then grips his right arm with his left hand behind his back. On a signal, they hop at each other, each trying to force the other out of the circle or to let go of his raised foot. When a player lets go of his foot or arm or leaves the circle, he is eliminated.

30-YARD DASH. Place markers at start and finish lines 30 yards apart. All Cub Scouts race from the start to the finish line. Pick first, second, and third places. Use this and other fitness races and contests to help boys develop different muscles of the body.

ARM WRESTLE. Each boy tries to force his opponent's hand to the ground or raise his elbow without moving his own elbow. Try alternating hands.

STICK PULL. Contestants sit on the ground, facing each other, with the soles of their shoes braced. The winner must pull his opponent forward to his feet.

HOP, STEP, AND JUMP RELAY. Get the denner to help you lead this relay race. Divide the den into two groups and let each group practice the hop, step, and jump until each member can do it. Then conduct the game.

The first member of each team toes a mark and takes in succession a hop, a step, and a jump. The second player does the same, toeing the last heel mark of his teammate. Other members repeat the action. The team whose last player finishes in front wins.

WHEELBARROW RACE. Divide the den into pairs. One Cub Scout in each pair "walks" on his hands while the other holds his legs as they race to a turning point. Boys reverse positions, and new wheelbarrows race back on their hands to the starting line.

CRAB RELAY RACE. Dens line up for a relay. The first boy in each den crawls crab-style to a line 15 feet away, stands up, and returns to tag the next boy, who continues in the same manner.

ASTRONAUT'S TEST. You'll need two broomsticks 3 to 4 feet long for this game. Form the den into teams facing each other. At the signal "go," the first boy in each line runs to a spot in front of his line, stands the stick on end, places his forehead on it, does three complete turns, drops the stick, and returns to touch off the next boy in line. The team finishing first wins.

HOPPING RELAY. Boys line up for a relay. One from each team hops 25 feet on his left foot to a marker and hops back on his right foot to tag the next boy in line.

STRONG ARM TRICK. Show this skill to the boys in your den and suggest that they go home and try it on their family. This is done by holding the palm of each hand against the chest with fingertips touching. After the Cub Scout gets into this position, he should challenge an adult or another Cub Scout to pull his fingers apart, using only a steady pull.

KANGAROO HOP RELAY. Cub Scouts assume a semisquat position. Keeping their feet together, they spring forward to cover a set distance. The first team done wins the relay.

GORILLA RELAY. Cub Scouts spread their feet shoulder width, bend down, and grasp their ankles. They walk forward, keeping their knees extended and legs straight.

LEG WRESTLE. Two Cub Scouts lie right side to right side on their backs with their heads in opposite directions. They hook right elbows. When you count "one," they raise their right legs and touch them together, then lower them. At the count of "two," they repeat this action. At "three," they hook their right knees and try to turn each other over. The player who pulls the other one over is the winner.

PUSH BACK. Two boys stand back-to-back with arms linked. Begin the contest between two lines, 20 feet apart. The winner is the one who pushes his opponent back over the line.

BAREFOOT MARBLE RELAY. Form two relay teams, and have players remove their shoes and socks. The first boy runs to a line 15 feet away. He grasps a marble with the toes of each foot, and then returns with them to tag the next boy.

See the *Cub Scout Leader How-To Book* for more ideas.

Skits, Puppets, and Pantomimes

Skits

At the pack meetings, each den will have some responsibility. It might be a ceremony, a demonstration, or a skit.

Skits help Cub Scouts develop their self-confidence and independence. You can help Cub Scouts with skits in many ways. You can help them plan what they want to do, what characters they want to portray, and whether they will act the parts or create puppets.

The *Cub Scout Leader How-To Book* and *Cub Scout Program Helps* have many skit ideas. Ask one of your den leaders to let you review the ideas in these books. Also, the monthly theme will help stir the imagination.

Make skits real with props and costumes. Cub Scouts like to show off, and skits will help them do just that. Remember that they are not creating one-act plays, but rather short skits that last less than five minutes.

You can use several kinds of skits at pack meetings. One type is the *pantomime,* either with spoken narration or set to music, and another is the *puppet* show. With the den leaders, help the Cub Scouts decide how they want to develop their presentation.

Here is a simple outline and worksheet to help Cub Scouts develop their own original skits:

1. A boy wants something.

2. The boy starts to get it.

3. An obstacle stops the boy.

4. The boy achieves his goal.

You can use the worksheet on the next page to write down the skit ideas as the den members develop them. Use a large piece of paper and a marker so everyone can see what you write.

Some Skit Ideas

You can create comedy acts for almost any number of participants using the following skit ideas or one from your own imagination. Ask the Cub Scouts for ideas. They will have plenty of good ones. Get the boys together and have everyone work with ideas. In this way, a skit will develop quickly.

SKIT WORKSHEET

THEME OF SKIT _____

Plot: _____

_____

_____

_____

_____

_____

_____

Title: _____

Type of characters: People   OR   Puppets

_____   _____

_____   _____

_____   _____

_____   _____

_____   _____

Length of time: _____

Staging (lighting, sound effects, costumes, etc.):

_____

_____

_____

_____

_____

_____

_____

_____

_____

Characters (enough for everyone in the den):

_____

_____

_____

_____

_____

_____

_____

Location or setting: _____

What the character wants: _____

Obstacle or other problems to overcome: _____

_____

_____

_____

_____

_____

Crisis: _____

Ending: _____

_____

_____

_____

_____

_____

_____

AIRLINE FLIGHT. Passengers make funny remarks as they look out of the airplane. They mistake New York for Hawaii. They think that a small lake is the Atlantic Ocean (or the opposite). They mistake a bird for a space rocket. The flight attendant patiently corrects them.

BEACHCOMBERS. At the seashore, the players find all sorts of curious things on the beach, such as a bottle containing a letter written by Columbus and a pearl as big as a baseball.

AT THE ZOO. Players do and say funny things as they visit a zoo (with imaginary animals). A zookeeper tries to help them understand the animals.

LAUGH TIME. The actors show how many different ways there are to laugh. Some laugh with a deep rumble, others giggle, some roll on the floor.

SINGERS. Players hold a tryout for singing roles in a musical play. Each player sings briefly and humorously.

NATURE HIKE. Players are on a nature hike. They try to identify different kinds of birds and trees but get all mixed up.

CANDIDATES. Several candidates for office practice their speeches. The candidates make strange promises, such as a pair of fishing boots for everyone.

IMITATION CONTEST. Performers hold a contest to see who can give the best imitation. They imitate a puppet, a policeman, an animal trainer, and so on.

LOST WATCH. Someone has lost his watch at a picnic. Everyone has interesting adventures while searching for the watch. (Example: They chase a squirrel that they think has taken the watch.)

HOMEWORK. A player needs help in finding answers to his homework problems. His friends look through books for him. After all sorts of wrong answers, they finally come up with correct ones.

TELEVISION SHOP. Customers come into the television repair shop to ask odd questions about their sets. For example, someone asks whether the trouble was in the carburetor or the spark plugs.

TREASURE HUNT. The performers have an old treasure map. They search around the desert and find old bottles and tires, but no treasure. Still, they have a good time.

STRANGE ISLAND. The skit takes place on a remote island where visitors run into all sorts of strange creatures. (You can "recycle" costumes and masks from other skits for this one.)

CANDY FACTORY. Workers in a candy factory try to invent new kinds of candy. They come up with green chocolates, square jelly beans, and other strange sweets.

GAS STATION. A motorist in an imaginary car drives into an imaginary gas station. Attendants rush out to sell him tires, oil, a battery, and anything else they can. They even try to charge him for air in his tires.

During den meetings, you may help the Cub Scouts prepare their costumes or other props. They will also rehearse their skit one or more times. At the pack meeting, you should help them get their props and costumes ready so they will be prepared when it is time for their presentation.

Puppets

Puppets are fun to make and use. Puppets help Cub Scouts improve their voice projection, gain self-confidence, and develop creativity. If boys are shy about being in front of a crowd at pack meetings, puppets give them a way to take part without actually standing before an audience.

Cub Scouts can make many different kinds of puppets. You will be able to help the Cub Scouts make their puppets as well as develop their puppet skit. They will also need to create a stage for their puppet show. Perhaps you can also help them find some background music for their show.

FOLD-UP PAPER PUPPET. This simple puppet will give Cub Scouts a chance to practice "being someone else" and to learn to move the puppet's mouth to fit the words being spoken.

1. Fold a sheet of construction paper into thirds lengthwise.

2&3. Fold the paper into quarters with the top and bottom meeting in the middle.

4. Fold in half with the openings on the outside.

5. Slip thumb and fingers into slot to make the puppet "talk."

Decorate with a different color of construction paper, felt, marking pens, yarn, etc.

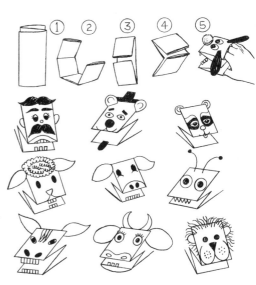

Pantomimes

Pantomime is an expression of a thought, emotion, or action without words. In some forms, words may be supplied by a narrator or there may be recorded music, but the actors never speak.

Encourage the Cub Scouts to think about how any thought or feeling or action can be shown without words. Have the boys think about how they would act, and then have them get up and show how they would do it. Here are some ideas:

Show how you would walk if . . .

- You had to go into a room where a baby was sleeping
- You were wearing skis
- You were on stilts
- You had a nail in your shoe
- It was very hot
- It was very cold
- You were scared
- You were happy

Show how you would look if . . .

- Someone gave you a ferocious lion
- Someone gave you a beautiful ring
- You lost something . . . and found it again!
- You slipped on ice
- Your report card was all "A's"
- You smelled something bad
- You tasted something you didn't like

Pantomime the five senses:

Hearing   A sudden clap of thunder
                 A far away bell
                 A whisper
                 Dance music

Seeing	A friend approach
	An auto crash
	A house on fire
	A bird flying by
Tasting	Food to see whether it is properly seasoned
	Hot soup
	Bitter medicine
Feeling	Fresh paint
	Sandpaper
	Waves on a beach
	Warmth from a stove
Smelling	A dead fish
	Fresh flowers
	Your favorite meal

Show how you would act if you were a . . .

Baker	Actor	Policeman
Baseball player	Doctor	Boxer
Lawyer	Swimmer	Dentist
Singer	Plumber	Dancer
Barber	Band member	Scuba diver

The *Cub Scout Leader How-To Book* has two chapters on skits and puppets. Ask one of your den leaders to let you borrow a copy so you can review it for ideas. *Cub Scout Program Helps* may also have skit ideas.

Ceremonies

Ceremonies are used to open and close the den meeting and to mark special events in the lives of the Cub Scouts.

Remember these four things when planning den ceremonies:

1. Keep them simple.

2. Keep them short.

3. Fit them to everyday experiences.

4. Don't get in a rut.

Cub Scout Opening Ceremonies

Insist on proper courtesy and respect for the U.S. flag. Cub Scouts may complete a requirement for Wolf Achievement 2, "Your Flag," by leading a flag ceremony in the den.

- Have boys give the Cub Scout salute and repeat the Pledge of Allegiance to the flag.

- Have Cub Scouts march past the U.S. flag or den flag or both, saluting. Place the U.S. flag on the right.

- Parade the U.S. flag and den flag past a line of Cub Scouts, who stand at attention and salute.

- Plan a ceremony on the history of the flag. Each boy can make and color a different paper flag to show how our present flag was formed.

- Boys can put on a ceremony based on an historic person whose birthday is celebrated during the month the den meeting is held. For example, use Abraham Lincoln or George Washington for February.

- Read and have the den act out a simple story about one of these famous people.

Webelos Scout Opening Ceremonies

Boys need something that says to them "the meeting has now officially started." A simple opening ceremony accomplishes this. Webelos Scouts will soon be Boy Scouts, so use of the Scout Oath and Law in ceremonies will help them to better understand the real meaning of each. Here are a few simple opening ceremonies that you can use in your meetings.

- Pledge allegiance to the flag.

- Face the flag and in unison sing "America," "America, the Beautiful," or "God Bless America."

- Form a circle around the den flag, with Webelos Scouts grasping the flagpole with their left hands.

- Give the Cub Scout sign with right hands and repeat the Cub Scout Promise or the Scout Oath.

- Assign a point of the Scout Law each week to a Webelos Scout. Have him prepare to read the point of the Law at the opening of the next week's meeting and give a brief explanation of what it means.

- Form the den into a horseshoe formation, with the U.S. flag in front of the horseshoe. Each Webelos Scout in turn steps forward, salutes the flag, and steps back in formation. When all have finished, the den gives the Cub Scout Promise or Scout Oath.

- Line up the den in a single line. Bring Webelos Scouts to attention, and turn out all the lights. Spotlight the U.S. flag with a flashlight. One Webelos Scout reads the first verse of "The Star-Spangled Banner."

Other Ceremonies

NEW BOYS. Whenever a prospective Cub Scout visits your den, make him feel at home. Welcome him by having the denner introduce him to the den. Tell him about Cub Scouting and the den activities.

You and the den leader should invite him to bring his family to the next meeting of your pack. Probably, the boy will know some of your den's members and will be able to feel right at home after a few meetings.

For a ceremony welcoming him into the den, you might form a Living Circle with the new member in the center and have all the Cub Scouts say the Promise and Law of the Pack.

BIRTHDAYS. Each time a Cub Scout has a birthday, your den can celebrate it in some special way. Perhaps the boy's family will provide special treats or a birthday cake with candles. As the birthday Cub Scout blows out the candles, the other members of the den form a circle around him. When the candles are out, the denner should lead the boys in a den yell.

THE LIVING CIRCLE. The Living Circle may be used alone or as a part of another ceremony. It reminds a Cub Scout of the fine friendships he is making in Cub Scouting.

Form the Living Circle by standing with the den leaders and den in a close circle, facing inward. Ask everyone to turn slightly to the right in the circle and extend his left hand into the center, palm downward and left thumb pointing to the right.

Have each boy grasp the extended left thumb of the person on his left—thus making a Living Circle as shown below. Each person should hold his right hand high above his head in the Cub Scout sign. Then everyone can repeat the Cub Scout Promise, Law of the Pack, or motto.

The Living Circle can be added to by pumping all the left hands up and down while the Cub Scouts say "Ah-h–kay-y-la! We-e-e'll do-o-o ou-u-r best!" Have everyone snap into a circle of individual salutes at the word "best."

ADVANCEMENT. Although the boys in your den will be recognized for their advancements and receive their badges at the pack meeting, don't miss the opportunity of holding a ceremony to honor these boys in front of the members of the den.

Begin the den advancement ceremony by reporting to the den the names of the Cub Scouts who are ready to go before the pack to receive their awards. Have them stand and say, "Let's show [names] we're proud of them."

Ask each of the boys receiving awards to tell other members of the den what he has done to meet the requirements for his badge. If your den has a flag, present this to the boy or boys to hold as the denner leads a cheer or yell. The yell may be practiced at this time so that it can be used at the pack meeting awards presentation.

IMMEDIATE RECOGNITION CEREMONIES. Before receiving a Wolf or Bear badge, a Cub Scout can earn an "immediate recognition" bead for completing four achievements. These beads are worn suspended from the Progress Toward Ranks emblem on the right pocket of the uniform shirt. They are presented in the den meeting. This is an opportunity to have a special ceremony for these Cub Scouts.

Stand in a circle with those Cub Scouts who are getting beads standing next to the den leaders. Each of the Cub Scouts may be asked to tell which achievements he completed and perhaps something about one special project. The denner then leads the den yell or the short grand howl.

GRAND HOWL. For special recognition ceremonies of guests, parents, leaders, and members of your den, use this version of the grand howl. It is longer than the short grand howl and includes more opportunities for action.

Boys stand in a circle. The person being honored stands in the center. Starting from a crouching position, the boys make the Cub Scout sign, but instead of putting their hands over their heads, they touch the ground between their feet with the two fingers of both hands. Then, wolf-like, they raise their heads and howl, "Ah-h–kay-y–la! We-e-e'll do-o-o ou-u-ur best!" As they yell the word "best" in unison, they jump to their feet, with both hands held high above their heads in the Cub Scout sign. Hands remain up while the den chief or den leader yells "Dyb-dyb-dyb-dyb" (meaning "do your best"). On the fourth "dyb," each boy drops his left hand smartly to his side, makes the Cub Scout salute with his right hand, and shouts "We'll dob-dob-dob-dob" (meaning "do our best"). After the fourth "dob," the boys drop their right hands to their sides and stand at attention.

SHORT GRAND HOWL. Have Cub Scouts form a circle around the person in whose honor the grand howl is to be given. This may be a visitor, a leader, or a Cub Scout who is being recognized.

Ask each Cub Scout in the circle to squat, make the two-fingered Cub Scout sign with each hand, and touch the fingers of both hands between his feet to the ground. Then lead the boys in a long howl, "Ah-h–kay-y–la! We-e-e'll do-o-o ou-u-r best!" As they yell the last word—"best"— have them jump to their feet, with both hands high above their heads in the Cub Scout sign.

Cub Scout Closing Ceremonies

A simple ceremony—based on the flag, our country's history, or patriotic songs—is a quiet and impressive way to close a meeting.

- Form your den around the U.S. flag or den flag. Have the boys salute and sing "God Bless America" or one stanza of "America."

- Turn off the lights in the meeting room, light the artificial campfire, and sing "America, the Beautiful."

- Play "America" as background music and read the Preamble to the Constitution of the United States or have Cub Scouts name the 13 original colonies, one by one.

- Ask boys to prepare in advance a 10-line statement on "What My Flag Means to Me." Your den leader can select an interesting one and have the author read it.

- Turn off the lights and shine the beam of a flashlight on the flag fluttering in the breeze of an electric fan. Sing "The Star-Spangled Banner."

- Form a friendship circle by giving each Cub Scout a 3-foot section of rope. Have them join ropes by tying a square knot to ropes on their left. Each boy holds his rope with his left hand and pulls back to form a tight circle. Remind them of the meaning of the friendship circle by saying: "You are now a part of a group of close friends, held together by the square knot—the symbol of trust. Let us give our Cub Scout Promise."

- Close your meeting with a short thought on the meaning of the Cub Scout motto, the Law of the Pack, or the Cub Scout Promise.

Webelos Scout Closing Ceremonies

The closing ceremony offers another chance for you to get across some of the ideas of the Boy Scouts of America—patriotism, mental alertness, and good citizenship. Here are a few closing ceremonies to try with the den.

- The den stands in circle with heads bowed. The leader gives the Scout benediction—"May the Great Master of all Scouts be with us until we meet again."

- The den forms a circle. Each boy crosses his arms in front of himself and grasps his neighbors' hands. Sing "Scout Vesper" from the *Boy Scout Songbook,* followed by humming "Taps."

- Retire the U.S. flag. Boys salute as the flag is retired. The leader says, "Be Prepared"; Webelos Scouts respond by shouting, "We'll Be Prepared."

- With lights dimmed, sing "Taps" from the *Boy Scout Songbook.* Each boy slowly raises his outstretched right hand with the change of lines "from the lake, from the hills, from the sky"; on "all is well," all arms are folded across chests and heads are bowed.

- Form a circle. Each boy makes the Scout sign with his right hand and with his left grasps the upraised right wrist of the boy to his left. The den chief gives each point of the Scout Law, and as each point is given, the Webelos Scouts repeat it.

- Form a brotherhood circle, with each boy placing his arms around the shoulders of the boy on each side. Sing "Scout's Good-Night Song" from the *Boy Scout Songbook.*

Ask your den leader to let you see *Cub Scout Ceremonies for Dens and Packs* for more ideas.

CHAPTER 6

Your
Service
Record

DEN CHIEF

Den Chief Service Award

Preparation

Before you begin work on this service award, discuss with your den leader and either your Scoutmaster or Cubmaster the role and importance of the den chief. Your discussion should include the following:

- The importance of the attitude of service within Boy Scouting

- The attitude regarding service within the den

- The attitude regarding service to the den leader

- The importance of the attitude regarding leadership within Boy Scouting

- The attitude regarding leadership within the den

- The length of service to the pack

- The need to purchase, carry, and use this book

Den Chief _____
Your name

has discussed the role of den chief with us and is now prepared to begin working for the award.

Scoutmaster or Cubmaster _____
Signature   Date

Den Leader _____
Signature   Date

Period of Service

Date/Leader's
Initials*

_____ Den chief has served the pack faithfully for one full year.

Training

_____ Attended den chief training (if available within year of service).

OR

_____ Was trained by the assistant Cubmaster and den leader.

*Leader may be the den leader, Cubmaster, or Scoutmaster.

Service Requirements

_____ **Know the purposes of Cub Scouting.** The den chief understands the purposes of Cub Scouting.

_____ **Help Cub Scouts achieve the purposes of Cub Scouting.** The den chief knows and uses the following within the den:

- The Cub Scout Promise

- The Law of the Pack

- The Cub Scout motto

- The Cub Scout salute

- The Cub Scout sign

- The Cub Scout handshake

- The meaning of *Webelos*

_____ **Be the activities assistant in den meetings.** The den chief has led the following activities:

- Five songs _____ _____ _____ _____ _____

- Five stunts or skits _____ _____ _____ _____ _____

- Five games _____ _____ _____ _____ _____

- Five sports activities _____ _____ _____ _____ _____

_____ **Set a good example by attitude and uniforming.** The den chief has maintained the following for a period of six months:

- A cheerful Scouting attitude within the den

_____ _____ _____ _____ _____ _____

- Proper uniforming at den meetings

_____ _____ _____ _____ _____ _____

_____ **Be a friend to the boys in the den.** The den chief understands the following:

*Leader may be the den leader, Cubmaster, or Scoutmaster.

- The meaning of friendship

- What Cub Scout–age boys are like

- The need to praise and build up the boys

_____ **Take part in weekly meetings.** The den chief took part in weekly meetings for six months.

_____ _____ _____ _____ _____ _____

_____ **Assist the den at the monthly pack program.** The den chief has assisted the den at the monthly pack program at least three times.

_____ _____ _____

_____ **Know the importance of the monthly theme.** The den chief has discussed the monthly theme and understands its importance.

_____ **Meet as needed with the adult members of the den, pack, or troop.** The den chief understands the need to work together. He has maintained a notebook (preferably the *Cub Scout Leader Program Notebook*) with the telephone numbers of the den leader, assistant Cubmaster who works with den chiefs, Scoutmaster, and any other adult member of the troop or pack named by the den leader. This notebook has been used to mark down the dates and times of all den functions for one year. The den chief has either attended the annual pack planning conference or met with the Cubmaster to prepare his notebook. The den chief has called the leaders concerned if unable to attend scheduled meetings.

Complete Four of These Projects

_____ Serve as a staff member of a Cub Scout special event, such as a Scouting show, bicycle rodeo, etc.

_____ Serve as a staff member of a Cub Scout day camp or resident camp.

_____ Advance one Boy Scout rank.

_____ Assist in recruiting three new Cub Scouts:

Names: _____

_____

_____

_____ Assist three Webelos Scouts to join a troop.

Names: _____

_____

_____

_____ Help to plan and carry out a joint pack-troop activity.

_____ Recommend to your Scoutmaster another Boy Scout to be a den chief.

Den Chief Service Award Approval

Den Chief _____

of Troop _____

has completed the preparation, service period, training, service requirements, and projects. He is therefore entitled to receive and wear the Den Chief Service Award.

Cubmaster _____
                        Signature   Date

Den Leader _____
                        Signature   Date

Show this to your Scoutmaster for presentation at the appropriate ceremony.

Scoutmaster _____

Date Awarded _____ Pack _____

Den Chief Service Award Recognition

Den chiefs who qualify for the Den Chief Service Award wear the special Den Chief Service Award Cord and may continue to wear it as long as they are Scouts, even if no longer a den chief.

After completing the requirements on pages 97–100, you will receive the Den Chief Service Award.

DEN CHIEF SERVICE AWARD

THIS IS TO CERTIFY THAT

_____

OF TROOP _____

HAS SERVED PACK _____ AS A DEN CHIEF

AND HAS MET THE REQUIREMENTS FOR THIS AWARD

_____
DATE

_____   _____
DEN LEADER OR   SCOUTMASTER
WEBELOS DEN LEADER

Index